I Talk to Myself a Lot

by
Audre Pitts

Beacon Hill Press of Kansas City
Kansas City, Missouri

Dedication

To my Cascade Manor friends
Who have learned the secret
Of increasing in wisdom
And stature—
While staying forever young
In their hearts.

Contents

1

Darling, I'm Not Growing Old

Darling, I'm not growing old;
  As to that let's be agreed;
Wisps of silver here and there
  Do not mean I've gone to seed.
But, my darling, I'll admit
  That I'm not quite as young and spry,
Nor near as nimble or as fit
  As I was in days gone by.

There are a few other things I could admit—and do so later in this book. And, of course, I'm growing older. It's the only way we *can* grow. Clocks don't run backward. They keep going "tick, tock," not "tock, tick."

But age, like beauty, is mostly in the eyes of the beholder. Some of my very young friends think I am old. My older friends think I am young.

While on an extended visit in Kansas a friend and I

went every two weeks to a rest home for a sing-along. Some of those dear people were so full of fun we'd often leave laughing heartily. They loved to sing. You should have heard them belt out "Old MacDonald Had a Farm." Sometimes they would start exchanging quips with us, and we'd all have a hilarious time. Most of them were in wheelchairs. Some were amputees. But their faces shone. Don't tell me they were old. Their bodies were, but they weren't.

I lived for several years at Cascade Manor—a retirement residence in Eugene, Ore. You should have been at some of our parties. I still love to visit with those dear "young" people whom some would label "old."

To My Doctor

You say my arteries are hard,
  That I am getting old;
My blood pressure is rising
  And my feet are always cold;
My eyes are dim, my ears are deaf,
  I more and more forget.
But don't call the mortuary, please;
  There's lots of life in these bones yet!

2

Help! My Arteries Are Hardening

My arteries began hardening the day I was born. There is no medical record of this, but it has to be true.

Some people *grow* senile. I was born that way. I've had "creeping senility" all my life—and now I think it's got me. I took early senility the way some people take early retirement.

When I married a farmer, I took over the job of planting a garden. When I asked him how deep I should dig the holes to plant cucumbers, he said, "Oh, about a foot deep." He expected me to know enough to fill it most of the way up first with fertilizer. (We had lots of the organic kind.)

Well, I dug the holes a foot deep, and I dropped the

11

little seeds clear to the bottom of the holes. Then I covered them up with 12 inches of plain old dirt.

Wonder of wonders! They did come up—the same year, too.

When I was a girl, my sister and I thought we'd found a surefire shortcut to beauty. Staring at us out of a magazine in big block letters were the words "Hair Pulling Makes You Beautiful." Eureka! With a shout of triumph I grabbed her long hair, and she took a fistful of mine. Oh, how we pulled. We wanted to be beautiful, and we wanted to be beautiful right then and there.

When the agony of pain finally made us call a halt, we read the rest of the article. It went on to say that *gently* pulling strands of your own hair would get rid of the dead hairs and zing up (my words, not theirs) the others. Phooey, we decided to let the dead hairs fall out by themselves, and the rest could make it on their own.

Some 30 or 40 years ago—in the days when ladies wore hats—I bought a new one and wore it out of the store. My next stop was at the bank. As I walked in, I met a lady whom I didn't know—but I smiled at her anyway. She smiled back. There was something about that smile that seemed familiar. I looked again. It was my reflection in a big mirror.

I have a chronic habit of locking myself out of the house. Usually, I have an extra key made and leave it with a neighbor. In one apartment, where I wasn't that well acquainted, I solved the problem by attaching a card to the extra key and tucking it under the doorsill where I—or anyone else for that matter—could easily find it. On the card I wrote a message:

> *Enter my house, take what you will,*
> *But please put the key back under the sill.*

I've moved again. (I *do* pay my rent!) I haven't had an extra key made yet. And I did it again—I locked myself out. I knew one window was partly open, but it was high off the ground and *much* too small for me to enter. So I enlisted the aid of a youngish gentleman in the apartment next to mine—a man I barely knew.

My sweet, little "88 years young" neighbor brought her step stool. The man pried off the screen and crawled through the window to open my door. He wasn't a small man—I had to kind of help *push* him through.

I'm glad I won't need a house key for my mansion in heaven. I'd probably lose it in outer space.

> *Dear God,*
> *I'm such a harem-scarem,*
> *Helter-skelter,*
> *Witless sort of woman;*
> *How can You ever use me*
> *In Your kingdom work?*
> *But You do—*
> *Sometimes.*
> *Thank You, God.*

3

I Can't Remember

There are so many things I can't remember—like turning off the heat under the teakettle, or making a telephone call that was really important, or birthdays.

I can't remember what the Sunday School lesson was about last week, but I can remember my first Sunday School lesson. I was seven years old and our family had moved into a farming community where there was a small, white frame church.

The lesson was about Christ's triumphal entry into Jerusalem. The teacher had made a small sandbox scene (I think it was really just dirt) with tiny cardboard houses. She used wee, cedar twigs to represent the palm branches. I was enthralled and in my heart I, too, sang glad hosannas.

That, to me, is still one of the most stirring accounts in the Bible.

I can't remember the name of that woman I met yesterday, but I can remember four-year-old Linda. I was ill at the time and one Sunday morning as I mounted the church steps, clinging to my husband's arm, I met Linda. It was her birthday, and she was proudly carrying a card which her Sunday School teacher had given her. Seeing me, she held out her cherished card, saying, "Here, Mrs. Pitts, you can have this because you are sick." I will always remember Linda.

I can't remember what the choir special was last Sunday, but I remember when one of the men fell down while getting off the riser during a break in the Christmas cantata. He tried to get up, but his foot had gone asleep and he couldn't stand. So he quickly scrambled out on all fours.

Fortunately no one in the congregation saw him. He was on the back row, which went out first, and so was shielded from view by the other rows.

I've forgotten a lot of revival meetings I've attended, but I remember the one in which I gave my life to Christ. The next morning, as I knelt beside my bed to pray, I felt God's presence very sweetly near. But I was not sure I could live like a Christian. So I crawled back into bed and told God that if He wanted me to go to heaven, He'd have to take me right then while I was ready to go. But He didn't take me, so I got up and started out on a beautiful journey with Him—a journey that has lasted more than 50 years. I'm glad I got out of bed. I'd have had bedsores by now!

I can't remember very many sermons that I've heard, but I remember the night the Baptist preacher swallowed a June bug. During the hot summer months (before air conditioning had been thought of), all the churches in our town united for outdoor evening services in the city park. The various preachers took turns bringing the messages.

That night my sister and I were on the front seat. We had seen a big, hard-shelled beetle circling around the preacher's head for some time.

Suddenly he sort of gulped, coughed, and cleared his throat and remarked nonchalantly, "Those June bugs are terrible—especially if you swallow one." Then he continued with his sermon.

Right now I can't remember if it was Isaac Newton or John Newton who got conked on the head with an apple and came up with the theory of gravity, but I remember the day I broached the subject to the pupils in my third grade classroom.

When I asked what kept us from falling off the earth, Johnny (that was really his name) promptly and confidently answered, "God and gravity!"

I've met a lot of people in the different churches where we have worshipped. Many of them I don't remember, but I remember one little lady who couldn't keep from dozing off during the sermon. At intervals she would wake with a guilty start and say "Amen," then go back to sleep.

I don't remember how it fit into his sermon, but one Sunday morning the pastor told about a man who was having lunch with his grandson. The boy had been chattering incessantly, until Grandpa finally told him not to say anything more until he'd finished his salad.

The grandson was quiet for a moment, then he exclaimed, "Grandpa!"

The grandfather said sternly, "Be quiet."

"But, Grandpa," the boy insisted—and was again hushed. After the third try the boy subsided into resigned silence. Grandpa swallowed the last bite of his lettuce, laid down his fork, and said, "Now you may talk."

The boy looked up. "It's too late, Grandpa," he said ruefully. "You already ate the worm."

Just as the minister delivered the punch line, this lady suddenly roused from her nap and chirped a loud "Amen!"

The preacher recovered and went on with the rest of his sermon while the lady went back to sleep. But the congregation choked with laughter.

I can't remember a lot of unimportant things . . . like what day it is, or where I put things . . . but I can remember important things like lightning bugs, playing "statue" with the neighbor kids, watching cloud pictures, and listening to the serenade of the cicadas on hot summer evenings.

I can remember the warmth of the old heating stove in the living room as my brothers and sisters and I crowded around it on winter evenings. (Has central heating taken away some of the family togetherness we once had?)

I can remember firecrackers and sparklers on the Fourth of July, and lots of candy and nuts at Christmas.

I remember the Christmas when I was five years old. We lived in the country, and there was a program at the schoolhouse. Several of my brothers and sisters were in the program.

A bachelor in the neighborhood always brought gifts for the preschool youngsters and put them under the tree. My gift was a beautiful bisque doll with black curls and "sleepy" eyes. She wore a red dress and I gave her the most beautiful name I knew—Florence.

And I can remember later Christmases when my small daughter's eyes sparkled and danced with the joy of giving me a gift . . .

> As my little girl played
> 'Neath the Christmas tree,
>   She lifted her head and smiled;
> And I saw the light
> Of the Christmas star
>   Shining there in the eyes of my child.

4

I Talk to Myself a Lot

I used to laugh at Mom for talking to herself. In later years I realized that she probably did it because none of her large brood ever gave her a chance to talk. We were too busy chattering ourselves.

Now, I talk to myself without shame. Sometimes when it may appear that I am talking to myself, I'm really not. I may be talking to a knife and fork . . . "Let's see now, I'd better get you out of the drawer." Or to the pencil sharpener . . . or any other inanimate object around the place.

And, a lot of times, I talk to God—as though He were right beside me. Which He is.

But there are times when I talk just to myself. I've heard that it's okay if you don't answer back. Then I'm not okay, for I do answer. If I want to work out a problem or discuss a situation in my life, I hold a verbal conference

18

with me, myself, and I. I discuss the pros and cons of the matter and reach a decision which is acceptable to the three of us.

If I think of a funny remark when I am alone, I say it. Then I laugh at it. Do you suppose I really *am* senile?

Or do I just enjoy talking to a brilliant conversationalist?

> *I talk to myself*
> *A lot . . .*
> *I laugh with me . . .*
> *Or at me . . .*
> *And sometimes*
> *Cry . . .*
> *But, most of*
> *The time,*
> *I'm sharing those talks*
> *With God.*
> *Thank You, God, for listening.*

5

Some Things Confuse Me

In fact, a lot of things confuse me. He who invented vending machines was aiming at a higher consumer IQ than mine. I can't even operate a stamp machine. When I put money in a parking meter (for a friend who's toting me around), I put dimes where the pennies belong. I feel like I deserve a Congressional Medal of Honor for having learned to use the coin-operated washer and dryer in the apartment laundry room.

Years ago when jukeboxes were a new thing, my sister and I were in a small cafe that boasted one. On its program list was a pretty, popular song, so I dropped in my nickel. But I failed to push the record selector; so, instead of listening to the music I wanted, we ate our hamburgers to the tune of "Mr. Zip Zip Zip."

Food vending machines defeat me. I either deposit the wrong coins or I poke the wrong button and out comes liverwurst instead of pastrami. Or out comes coffee instead of hot chocolate.

You want to know what I think? I think they hire very small, very prankish people to hide inside those machines to play tricks with my dimes and quarters ... and my pastrami sandwiches.

I don't like pay telephones, but I hate to pass by one without stopping to feel in the coin return to see if someone forgot his dime.

I was going to call my brother from a Los Angeles bus depot on my first visit to that large, noisy city. (He lived in Baldwin Park.) I laid the proper change out where I could grab it up in a hurry. (I'm always sure they will call the police or something if I don't get it deposited *fast.*)

Just as I dropped in the dime for the dial tone, I heard a loud voice resounding throughout the depot—"Audre Pitts, report at the desk, please."

What had I done wrong ... and how did they know my name? I knew there were all sorts of new electronic techniques, but I didn't know they could tell my name from the fingerprints on my dime.

I headed for the desk—*after* retrieving my dime. I was a little surprised that they let me have it back instead of turning it over to the FBI for evidence.

I arrived there somewhat out of breath. *You* just try running half a block through a crowded bus station, clutching three or four pieces of carry-on luggage which you won't put in a locker because you're too chicken to try to operate one—with a legion of imaginary gendarmes breathing down your neck. You'd be out of breath, too.

They were only paging me (I thought they were *accusing* me) because my brother had phoned to see if my bus had arrived. And while I'm on the subject of lockers in bus stations or airports, if I did put my belongings in one,

I'd probably forget them and ride off into the sunset without them.

Even banks nowadays have places outside where customers can deposit, withdraw, make payments, or do most anything except rob the place. All you have to do is play tiddledywinks with a few buttons, and a drawer pops out with your money in it. I tried it last summer with the aid of a patient brother-in-law. I got my money, but I thought I'd lose my hand at the wrist. The drawer was almost faster at withdrawing than my hand was.

Post offices have places where you can weigh your own packages, figure the cost, and get the proper denomination of stamps to mail them—all by knowing when and where to "deposit coins." This may be a good service for those who want to mail after hours, but for the price I'm paying for stamps, I feel that Uncle Sam owes me a little personal service!

Computers are phasing out a lot of former methods of doing things. One of these days I'm afraid they will even phase out me.

So much for computers. Form sheets to fill out are even a worse headache. I'll write you a poem any day of the week—any hour of the day or night. But just let someone hand me a sheet of paper covered with blank spaces for me to fill in, and I get a mental block.

I had to change my voter registration because of a change of address. I put down the wrong birth date. I got the year right, but the day of the month wrong. I must go back and correct it. As it now stands, I am four days older than I really am. That will never do.

When I worked as social director at the manor where I lived, I had no problem performing my duties. In fact, everyone told me I was pretty good at the job. All but filling out my time card. The bookkeeper had to help me almost every month. And all I really had to do was write down four hours, five times a week.

Then there are the times I get all the blanks filled in correctly (without having to erase) in *writing*. Then I see where it reads, "Please *print* clearly."

ODE TO A BUS STOP VENDING MACHINE

Insert coins here,
Pull out lever,
Out comes a sandwich—
Isn't that clever?

But when I try it,
It just isn't funny;
I get no sandwich
And lose my money.

I'm not really starved;
So, if worse comes to worst,
I'll munch on the 'tater chips
Stashed in my purse.

6

Could You Tell Me Where...?

My ophthalmologist tells me I have excellent vision—with my glasses on, of course. If that is so, then why can't I see an item in the grocery or department store when it is right in front of my eyes? I'm always asking clerks, or customers, or anyone else within earshot, "Can you tell me where ...?"

I'm so short that it wasn't until quite recently that I discovered the overhead signs above the aisles. Even so, they are so high I almost fall over backward trying to read them.

One day I was wanting to board a city bus, but I couldn't find the designated stop sign. I knew right where there *had* been one, but it was gone. I decided to take a chance on the bus stopping for me anyway. It did. As I boarded it, I asked the driver, "What has happened to the sign that used to be here?"

He said, "Lady, you were standing right under it."

How many of God's signs and wonders do you suppose I've missed because my spiritual vision was out of focus or I hadn't set my sights high enough spiritually?

Verbal directions go right over my head, too. I feel like a mouse in a maze when I try to follow them.

I'm still worse at *giving* directions than I am *following* them. A young marine stopped at our home in California, asking directions to the home of a family in the neighborhood. It was a very small community, and there were no street signs. I carefully instructed him to "go straight down the road, to the first corner and turn right. At the next corner, turn left. There are two houses there and it is the other one."

He looked puzzled, and my daughter started laughing. Then she told me what I'd said.

Dear God,
It is sometimes
Hard for me
To find the things I want
In stores;
They seem to hide
From me
Until someone
Points them out.

But, when I come
To You,
You always
Help me find
Forgiveness,
Love,
Joy,
And peace
Beyond description.
Thank You, God.

25

7

I'm Always Getting Lost

It is hard to believe that an object my size could be lost so easily. But then it isn't others who lose me—I'm always losing myself—or my way.

When my husband and I would go on trips together, we often traveled at night. One night—in the late, late hours—we stopped at a gas station in a small logging community. I rubbed the sleep out of my eyes and stumbled over to the attendant.

"Where's the ladies' room?" I mumbled, and he pointed in a certain direction.

That's funny, I thought, having it in a separate building.

But I groggily made my way toward it. I opened the door into pitch darkness; and before I could feel for a light switch, I heard a clock ticking! That woke me up! I'd almost walked in on a sleeping logger.

Once I got completely lost in the hospital when I went to visit a couple of friends. I'd have made it all right, I *think,* if the first friend hadn't told me a shortcut to take to the wing where my other friend's room was.

(Beware of shortcuts. My husband would occasionally take them when we were traveling. We invariably ended up on a road that just quit—right in the middle of the woods. If all the unsuccessful shortcuts we've taken were laid end to end, they'd make a very long cut.)

But to get back to my friend—come to think of it, I never did reach her. By the time I found her room—asking directions from about every nurse in the halls—they'd taken her to surgery. So I was back in the world of endless corridors again. I had just about given up ever finding the lobby when I spied our pastor boarding the elevator. I leaped in behind him, and we went to the little sitting room where the friend's family was waiting for her to come out of surgery.

I should have left when he did, but I was talking and so I lost my guide. But the folks told me the lobby was just around the corner, so again I ventured forth. Would you believe it? I got lost again. I'd been in that building many times—all over it in fact. But that day I never saw anything or any place that looked even vaguely familiar. The woman's husband finally spotted me wandering around and took pity on me. He *led* me by the hand to the lobby. If it hadn't been for him, I'd probably still be haunting the halls.

Isn't that the way it is when a person is lost without Christ? Wandering helplessly—so near and yet so far. May I be ready to offer a helping hand as did my friend's husband that day.

> *I lose myself quite*
> *Easily;*
> *But someone comes*

27

Along
And shows me
The way I ought to go.
I remember, God,
When I was **really** *lost . . .*
You sent Your Son,
And He not only
Showed me the way . . .
He **is** *the Way.*
Thank You, God.

8

I Know I Put It Somewhere

Most places of business have a lost and found department. It's different at my house. I have a lost and never-found department.

The things which eventually are found show up in the strangest places—toothpicks in the refrigerator; macaroni (uncooked) in the sewing machine drawer . . .

Some things, I am convinced, simply vanish into thin air on their way to never-never land and are never seen again.

I live in a studio apartment—from choice. Now when I lose something, I at least know which room I lost it in.

The biggest thing I ever lost was a television set. But that wasn't my fault. Somewhere on the long, long trail a-winding from Kansas to Oregon last June, it disappeared from the moving van. The man at the warehouse in Salina said it was very definitely loaded on the truck. The invoice showed it so. But the driver claimed he had not unloaded anything before he got to Eugene—and it wasn't there. This is September and they are still trying to trace it.

I'm glad it was the TV instead of my jar of peanut butter.

One of my most embarrassing moments (I've had many) was when I lost my power of speech. There have been subsequent times when I've wished I had. But I'd just as soon it hadn't happened that one time.

I had gone to hear Payne Ratnor speak. He was governor of Kansas at that time—a jillion years ago. After he had finished speaking, I went, along with a crowd of others, to shake hands with him. I thought it might be kind of an honor to shake a governor's hand. The most prestigious person I'd ever shaken hands with was the preacher. But I never expected the governor to *say* anything.

As he took my hand, he thanked me graciously for coming to hear him. I wanted to make a gracious reply— but, gracious, my tongue wouldn't function. All I did was stand there and gabble, "Uh—ee—oh—ee—ah—ah—uh— ooh—ooo" with all the proper inflections—just no words. Translated, it meant, "I'm very glad to meet you, too."

Years later, while working at Cascade Manor, I met Congressman John Dellenback of Oregon, who was having lunch there. I was introduced as the hospitality chairman; but that wasn't my real title, so dumb old me had to set the record straight. I said, "No, I'm not the hospitality chairman. I'm the—the—the—" And my mind went blank. I looked frantically from one to another of the three people with whom I was lunching. But they were looking as blank as my mind felt. I finally blurted out, "I really can't remember *what* I am." He smiled and said, "Oh, that's all right."

Oh, dear, I knew he thought I was completely vacant upstairs. I should have let it rest at that. But suddenly—a light. I remembered! I tugged at Mr. Dellenback's coat sleeve as he stood near the table visiting with a friend (who happened to be my boss!) and said triumphantly, "Now I know what I am. I'm the social director."

If I had said I was Napoleon's wife, he couldn't have looked at me with more compassion. So I "up and told" him about my earlier experience with the governor of Kansas and told him that politicians always affected me like that. We laughed over it then—but I still cringe when I remember it.

I'm glad God can look down into my heart and know what I'm trying to say to Him when I pray. Because some of my prayers get as mixed up as my conversations.

> *I lose my thimble,*
> *I lose my thread;*
> *I've even been known*
> *To lose my head.*
>
> *I lose my socks,*
> *I lose my shoes;*
> *I lost most everything*
> *A person could lose.*
>
> *Of things I lose*
> *There seems no end,*
> *But God grant that I*
> *Never lose a friend.*

9

Your Old Persons Shall Dream

A dream is
A thought,
A hope,
A wish,
A prayer . . .
A dream is
A tapestry
Which the mind weaves
In its spare time.

When onlookers see me staring off dreamily into space, they are apt to label me as a senile old lady who is dreaming of the past. They don't realize that I'm still expecting a lot from the future!

I've always been a dreamer. I dreamed my way through childhood—with help from a sister whose imagination outdistanced even mine. We held "plike" (our shortened version of "play like") sessions which were literally out of this world.

We were gifted in the art of escapism. In our realm of make-believe we were always fabulously rich. We wore beautiful gowns of silk and velvet—and a sheer material we saw pictured in a catalog. We called it "Creep de chine"—(long *i*, "ch" as in *choo choo*).

If we were children today, I suppose we would be dreaming of faded blue jeans and permanent-wrinkle shirts!

We never lived in houses. In fact, we never just *lived* at all. We *dwelt* in huge palaces and dined (we never just *ate*) from shiny, gold plates . . . and were pampered within an inch of our imaginary lives.

We even chose different names for ourselves, which we changed as fancy directed. At one time we lifted the words *victim* and *item* from a spelling lesson. Presto, I became Helen Victims (I had no idea what it meant) and she was Fern Items. At still another time, one of us (I can't remember which) chose the name of Juanita. Only we pronounced it "Jew-Anta." We read a lot, but we didn't know Spanish or French pronunciations.

We hobnobbed with kings and queens. In fact, all of our imaginary friends were royalty.

As an adolescent (*teenagers* hadn't been invented yet), I was a starry-eyed romantic. I wove a beautiful dream about myself and the Prince of Wales—thoughts which I didn't even share with my sister. We were too old for "plike" then, but I was hooked on it.

It has never been clear to me how I spanned the distance from a small Kansas town to merry olde England. That is the beauty of daydreams—anything can happen.

In my reverie he became King of England; but, for love of me—a commoner—he gave up his throne.

Was I ever surprised when, some years later, all of this

33

really happened—except another American woman was the heroine!

By that time I was happily married to a "commoner" and wouldn't have traded places with her. She was welcome to my daydream. I'm sure he never knew he had married the wrong woman!

Having outgrown my Prince of Wales fantasy, I lowered my sentimental sights and started looking around me to see what my real world had to offer. Sure enough—one evening—wham! There he was—Prince Charming. He wasn't on a white charger. He wasn't wearing shining armor—or whatever Prince Charmings are supposed to wear. He was just there—and I can't even remember if he was wearing a suit or a pair of overalls. My Prince Charming lived on a farm.

We dreamed a lot of daydreams together—before and after we were married. Some came true. Some didn't. But the dreaming of them drew us closer together.

As a housewife I logged a lot of miles on my magic carpet as I zoomed over strange lands and exotic isles while my hands were busy with more mundane chores. This wasn't always a good idea. Once I put vanilla, instead of vinegar, in deviled eggs. Yuk!

As a mother I shared my flights of imagery with my daughter. Make-believes when she was a child—deeper dreams as she grew to young womanhood.

I still haven't kicked the habit, albeit my dreams are woven of sturdier and more common material than the star-spangled, silken gauze of yesteryears.

My grandson is the same age as the present Prince of Wales, heir to the British throne. So *that's out!*

And not even in my wildest flights of fancy can I imagine any Prince Charming being able to drag (much less swing) me up on his horse. If he did, the poor horse would collapse. And I don't want my daydreams cluttered up with dead horses.

I'm just not Princess Charming material. For one thing, there's too much material.

But now my dreams go far beyond the limits of this present world. I don't really know a lot about how it will be in heaven. But I like to believe I'll be reunited with my own Prince Charming there.

I know there will be "neither marrying nor giving in marriage," but I have a sneakin' hunch we'll still like each other a lot.

And I know that I will see the King of Kings! If the Revelation description of the Holy City is at all literal, it will far surpass all my childhood fantasies. I may not get to wear a "Creep de Chine" robe—but I will be clothed in His righteousness!

> *Heaven . . .*
> *What will it be?*
> *Its shining glory*
> *I cannot conceive . . .*
> *But this I know,*
> *My Savior will be there,*
> *His nail-scarred hand*
> *Outstretched to me . . .*
> *And that will make it*
> *Heaven.*

10

I Can't Recall Your Name

I envy people who can meet someone once and remember his name ever after. I've tried everything. I concentrate carefully, and repeat the name when I acknowledge the introduction. A few minutes later it's gone.

I've tried word association. We moved to a small community in Oregon, and on my first visit to church I was introduced to several Browns and several Thrushes. So I thought, "Brown Thrush."

That worked pretty well except it took a few weeks to separate the Browns from the Thrushes.

I was also introduced to a couple whose last name was Buck. We had just moved from the mountains of northern California where there was lots of buckbrush. So I thought, "Hm-m—Buckbrush!"

Then I had a problem. I couldn't remember if they were Mr. and Mrs. Buck or Mr. and Mrs. Brush.

A few years later we moved to another town (I have a pair of gypsy feet). In a year or so, these folks moved there, too. When they started coming to church, I laughingly told the pastor about the mixup I'd had with their name.

One Sunday at the close of the evening service, the pastor said, "Brother Bush, would you close in prayer?"

All was silence . . . and I was groaning inwardly. I realized I had confused our minister about the name, also. Only he remembered it as Bush instead of Brush.

He repeated, "Brother Bush . . . ?" Again silence. Finally the pastor himself prayed the benediction.

Even if I know a person well, I can't always come up with the name. I was trying to introduce a very good friend of mine one day. I gave the names of the other people all right, but my mind was a complete blank where hers was concerned. Finally, I expostulated, "Well, you know your name. Tell them who you are!"

My husband's niece and her family were visiting from out of state. As I was returning thanks at the table, I asked God to "bless Arlene and Jack and Garry and—and—and what's her name."

I couldn't think of Jeannie to save my neck—and I didn't want dinner to get cold.

Mom used to "call the roll" every time she wanted any of us. My father didn't always recognize us—away from home. One day my sister and I went into a grocery store. Papa courteously held the door for us as he was coming out. We knew he didn't recognize us so we kept still—until we got home that evening.

If you had 13 children, are you real sure you would know them all if you saw them away from home—with clean faces and hair combed? He did have kind of poor eyesight, too.

Aren't we glad our Heavenly Father doesn't have those human limitations? He knows us each by name, and He never gets mixed up. The love of parents is wonderful—but God's love is even greater.

I can't recall your name,
But I remember
How you smiled at me . . .
It warmed my heart
And made my day
Much happier.
I wish I could
Recall your name,
But, since I can't,
I'll cherish the memory
Of your smile.

11

God Bless My Bloopers

I'm afraid most of my bloopers aren't blessable. All I can do is take them to the Lord in prayer. But, once in a long while, one may happen which He can use.

He used someone's blooper to get me started writing the book *Let My Life Sing*. Tim LaHaye had spoken in our church that evening. He had books to sell, one of which was entitled, *How to Be Happy Though Married*.

After the service I was telling the pastor and his wife how much I had enjoyed the message. He said, "I think you would enjoy his books, too." Someone in passing (I don't even know who it was for sure) said, "Which one, *How to Be Happy Though Married*?" then went on her way.

She was only thinking of the humorous title, but I felt like I'd been kicked in the stomach by a mule. And I remarked, "Well, I could tell how to be happy even if you have to be alone." And then even more vigorously, "I could even write a *book* about *that*."

The pastor nodded and said, "I believe you could." And his wife agreed, "I'm sure you could."

So we decided on the spot that I should write a book. Just like that!

By the time I reached home, my confidence had waned considerably. In fact, it was almost nil. I decided I would just tell them that I couldn't do it (because I knew I couldn't) and that would end the matter.

The next day I attended an outdoor potluck at a friend's house. She was gathering flowers for a centerpiece and handed me some nasturtiums to hold while she was clipping others. I felt a bit of stinging in my palm, so I put my handkerchief (I'm still old-fashioned enough to use real ones away from home) under the flowers and it was okay.

At least I thought it was okay. It was a hot day—about 95 degrees—and I kept using the same hanky to wipe the perspiration from my face and neck. I took off my glasses and wiped around my eyes—not once, but many times. And later, when eating fried chicken, I used it as a napkin to wipe my mouth.

Oh, what a mess. I developed the most vicious allergy poisoning I've ever had—worse than poison oak had ever been.

I couldn't go anywhere, so, to keep from scratching, I wrote the book. Part of the time my hands were swollen so badly I could hardly hold a pen, and my eyes were mere slits. This, in spite of the medication I was taking.

But, as a result of one friend's blooper and another friend's nasturtiums, a book was born. Without the allergy, it is doubtful that the Lord could have kept me home long enough to write it.

Before starting on this one, I promised Him I would

stay home—at least part of the time—and write, if only He would protect me from allergies and friends.

Then, there was that night in prayer meeting a few years back. The pastor had said we would spend a few minutes at the beginning of the service to elect one member to the Youth Council. No one will ever be able to explain how it happened, but things really got snafued. Before one motion could be cleared, two or three amendments and motions were presented, and people were discussing the issue without addressing the chair. Things were in such a state of confusion you could even feel tensions mounting.

I felt so sorry for our pastor. It wasn't his fault at all. It got so ridiculous that it began seeming funny to me. I sat there chuckling to myself, thinking how glad I was that it wasn't *me* up there.

Just then the pastor said, "Well, we've used up all of our prayer meeting time—it's time for choir practice. We'll have to take care of this another time. Let's stand and, Audre, will you pray the closing prayer?"

Audre!—that was *me*! I wished I were somewhere else—anywhere else. I gulped down the chuckle that had become an instant lump of fright, and began. I don't remember all I said (maybe it is just as well), but I somehow managed to tell God and all the people that we loved our pastor even if he didn't know much. That wasn't what I meant to say at all. He was—and still is—a very intelligent man. But the preacher said a loud "Amen" and the crowd snickered.

I struggled on, realizing that the lump in my throat now was really my *foot*. After I'd made another dumb remark or two, the preacher said an even louder "Amen." (He was enjoying it.) The crowd laughed out loud. Before I was finished, they were literally guffawing! I wished God would take me to heaven right then and there.

41

I finally had sense enough to just quit trying. Then the people gathered around me—hugging me—patting me on the back. You'd have thought I'd just done something great instead of making a fool out of myself.

"That was exactly what we needed," they kept saying. "It broke the tension."

True—the tension was gone. But why me, Lord?

Dear God,
My tongue doesn't
Always say
The things I want
To say.
Somewhere
Between my brain
And my tongue tip
The words become
Scrambled . . .
Like alphabet soup.
But You know them,
You can read them . . . and,
Deep down in my heart,
They are beautiful.
Thank You, God.

12

I Must Have Left It

My husband often told me I needed a keeper. He was right. It was he who always gathered up my belongings for me after church—or any place else we happened to be. He accused me of trying to plant handkerchiefs, the way I scattered them around. "You know they won't grow," he'd chide me.

Now my friends sort of help look after me. In spite of their efforts I still manage to leave my wrap or umbrella or anything I might have with me. I've left packages in phone booths and at bus stops. I've had to yell, just as the bus was pulling away from the curb, "Wait! I left my package." They waited, and I was the gamut of many pairs of eyes while I hurried off the bus, retrieved my package, and again climbed aboard.

I've left packages in stores. I've left my purse numerous times in various places. Strangely enough, I very rarely ever lose things completely. Somehow they get returned to me.

Once I even left my small daughter at a friend's house where I had gone to visit. She went outside to play with the children in the backyard. When it came time to leave, my sister and I went out through the *front* yard. When we were several blocks away, I exclaimed in horror, "I forgot Dorothy Jeanne!"

One night I left an empty cardboard box on someone's porch. But I did that on purpose. My sister and I had gone with my daughter while she delivered May baskets. We were carrying them in the box. We had finished and were going home when we passed the home of a former teacher of mine. She hadn't been one of my favorite teachers. So I sneaked up on the porch and placed the big, empty box right in front of her door. Then we scooted.

We were almost home when I remembered that it was a box I'd had something shipped to me in—my name and address were clearly printed on it!

"Be sure your sins will find you out."

> *I left my shawl at church;*
> *I left my purse there, too.*
> *I'm always leaving things behind;*
> *I don't know what to do.*
>
> *I spoke a kind word to a child;*
> *I smiled and went my way;*
> *I left a little bit of joy*
> *To brighten someone's day.*
>
> *I know I am forgetful,*
> *But this I want to do . . .*
> *While spreading my belongings,*
> *I'll spread some sunshine too.*

13

Have I Told You This Before?

Repeating myself may not be a sign of advancing age, but I'm beginning to wonder. I try to console myself by saying it is because I have so many friends that I can't remember which ones I've already told my very interesting (?) news—and I don't want to miss anyone.

Ergo . . . my most frequently asked question is: "Have I told you this before?"

I have a brother who spikes his listeners' guns by warning, "I've probably told you this a million times, but . . . "

After all, we listen to some of the same songs over and over . . . and read a poem more than once. And some of us have favorite books which we've reread many times.

So why can't I tell my stories over and over and over and . . .?

I find myself repeating myself,
  It irks one very sore;
It seems I'm always saying,
  "Have I told you this before?"

People are mostly too polite
  To tell me right out plain—
But sometimes on their faces I see
  A look of patient pain.

But it doesn't really matter, for
  If I want to tell it—why then,
I don't care if I've told you before—
  I'm going to tell it again!

14

What Day Is It Today?

My sister once told of a little lady who lived near them when their children were small. Every day as the youngsters would pass this neighbor's house, she would meet them at the gate and sweetly ask, "What day is it today, boys?"

I know just how she felt. I'm lucky if I remember what month it is. A few years ago I went through a phase when I dated all my checks the wrong *year*—each one a *different* wrong year.

One summer when I had been helping in VBS, I came home on Friday afternoon and collapsed in an exhausted heap on the bed. I went to sleep and later woke up feeling fit as a fiddle. I glanced at the clock—8:30. I'd slept all night! I got up, ate breakfast, wrote a letter (dated Saturday a.m.) and was well into my Saturday cleaning when I noticed it was getting cloudy. Soon it got so dark I had to turn on the lights. All the neighbors had theirs on, too.

I kept muttering to myself that there must be a bad storm brewing. I turned on TV to see if there were any local storm warnings. The TV programs were all mixed up. The only ones I could get were the ones that were usually on the night schedule.

After some time it broke in upon my consciousness that I had wakened at 8:30 *Friday evening*—not 8:30 *Saturday morning*, as I had thought.

Then I had to turn my mental time clock back 12 hours and finish up Friday before I could have Saturday.

What day is it today?
Time moves so swiftly;
Clocks run faster than
When I was younger,
I am sure.
And calendars
Must have fewer pages.
Small wonder that
I must keep asking . . .
Oh, yes, I remember . . .
"This is the day
Which the Lord hath made,
I will rejoice
And be glad in it!"

15

I Have This Pain

Oh yes, we all do; and if we can find a listening ear, we will probably tell about it in great detail.

I often ride the city bus, and I've heard graphic descriptions of every sickness imaginable as I've caught snatches of conversations among the other passengers.

I call it "swapping symptoms" when I hear a group of people taking turns telling about their ailments—and their operations.

A minister friend once told me I could never give an "organ recital," because I'd never had surgery.

But I have this constant pain in my shoulder—and a creaky knee; and then there was the time I was poisoned by some nasturtiums . . .

> *You have a pain? Well,*
> *I have one, too . . .*
> *I know mine's worse*

'Cause it makes me blue.
Come, dear friend, tell me—
Now is the time—
You tell me your aches,
And I'll tell you mine.

16

I Used to...

Do any of these remarks sound familiar?

"I wish you could have tasted *my* cooking. I used to fix the best . . ."

"I was known as the best housekeeper in the country. People used to say they could *eat* off my floor." (Did they offer to, though?)

"I used to make the most beautiful flower arrangements—but, oh no, I won't do it now."

"My flowers were the most beautiful in town. Of course, now—"

I'm always slightly amused when I hear things like this. Of course, part of it may be envy because I don't have too much to brag about.

After years of practising on a patient husband (whose

mother really was the best cook in the neighborhood), I managed to do reasonably well. But it's a wonder I didn't kill off my family in the process of learning.

I sewed for myself and my daughter. I thought I did pretty well until I helped her with a dress she was making for a school project. She flunked the course—and I gave up sewing.

I never could iron well—we won't even talk about that.

I gradually got to be a pretty good (not excellent—just pretty good) housekeeper. I was a vigorous one, at least. My husband considered me a very noisy housekeeper. When I ironed, I set the iron down with a resounding thump. When I washed dishes, I rattled pots and pans with a vengeance—and clattered cups and saucers with serene disregard for breakage. I hardly ever broke any, though.

He hated the whir of the vacuum cleaner and would have sworn under oath that I ran the washer and dryer night and day, six days a week—for two people! He even thought I could be noisy using a dust cloth, I think.

I tried to do most of my work when he was gone. This wasn't easy, since he worked on the night shift a lot and was home during the day. It made a night owl out of me, too. I'm still one.

Sometimes I think I would like to be a well-disciplined person with a well-organized schedule. But I'm not.

I might do better at it if it were not for my penchant for writing poetry. Why is it that the urge to write comes when I should be doing something else? Why can't the muse be a well-behaved muse and make his appearance at more convenient times?

But—no! Anyone who has done any writing at all knows that the muse is not always a friend. Sometimes he is a tyrant who steals sleep from you at night and drives you in search of pen and paper as frantically as an addict looking for a fix.

He can take away your desire for food—keeping you writing far beyond your regular mealtime, even making you skip meals entirely. (With me that isn't really tyranny. It's a benevolent miracle.)

Sometimes *she* is a siren who whispers softly in your ear, even in church when you really *want* to be listening to the sermon.

Other times she comes as a playmate who beckons you to leave the dishes, the bed, the whole works—and you do. Because if you don't, your playmate will skip away, taking all her ideas and inspiration with her.

Whatever the disguise, I am often caught without pen and paper. I buy pencils practically by the gross, ballpoint pens fascinate me, and I can't pass up a memo pad or notebook in any store. I fill my purse with a generous supply of all these. But I also fill it with a lot of other necessities.

Last Sunday we had tent services on our new church property. It had rained all week and I was afraid it might be muddy, so I tucked a pair of plastic overshoes in the bottom of my purse. (I was carrying a big purse that day.) At least, I intended to put them on the bottom but it turned out that they were on top of my wallet. I had an awful time getting my tithe check out without everyone seeing my overshoes (which I didn't need after all).

But, anyway it takes time (days sometimes) to find what I want.

So a lot of my poems are just written "in my head." My brain is a veritable clutter of unwritten, deathless poetry and deadly prose. If it were all put on paper, I'd probably toss most of it in the wastebasket anyway.

Perhaps I'd better let other people reminisce about

their past deeds of glory. Mine weren't—and still aren't—
all that glorious.

> *Nostalgia*
> *Is a memory*
> *Wrapped in rose-tinted mist*
> *Which time*
> *And imagination*
> *Have painted*
> *With even more*
> *Brilliant colors*
> *Than the*
> *Original.*

17

Before I Forget

A year ago I worked on a committee with members of my high school graduating class in my hometown of Concordia, Kans. We were planning our 50-year reunion. More fun!

We spent a lot of time looking through old yearbooks together—laughing at half-forgotten incidents of those long-ago days. We laughed even more at ourselves trying to get things organized.

We jotted down all the ideas which were presented—if we could find our pens or paper. If we didn't get it written down, we forgot it. Every so often we'd misplace our notes—but we found them again—after a lot of shuffling.

Our discussions were punctuated with, "Oh, before I forget . . ." or "While I'm thinking of it . . ." or "While

I've got it and it's still mine, let me say it . . ." If we waited, we forgot what we wanted to say. So we had to interrupt—or forget it. The crazy part was that when we interrupted to share *our* bright idea, we made the other fellow forget *his*.

Our chairman (chairperson?) kept saying, "What I miss most is my mind." She still has a lot more left than some of us started out with.

The reunion was perfect! We'd never had one before, but 39 of us—plus spouses for some—came from several states. And everyone wanted to see everyone else.

It was better than if we could have really turned the clock back, because all my classmates are even nicer now than when we were young. And they have such nice husbands and wives. I wish I hadn't forgotten to tell more of them so.

> *Before I forget,*
> *I want to say*
> *I love You, God;*
> *I want to thank You, too,*
> *For loving me.*
> *So many things*
> *I need to say*
> *Before I forget—*
> *How very much I love*
> *My friends,*
> *And how very much I cherish*
> *Their love for me.*
> *Help me to tell them, God,*
> *Before I forget.*

18

Growing Up or Growing Old?

Am I growing up—or just growing old?
Growing old sometimes means:
 Aches and pains,
 forgetting more and more,
 gradually losing family and old friends,
 moving to smaller quarters
 and giving up cherished belongings,
 reduced income,
 repeating myself more often.
But growing up means:
 speaking to someone instead of turning a cold
  shoulder,
 listening with kindness (if not intense interest) to an
  anecdote I've heard so often I could tell it better
  myself,
 smiling—even when I feel like glowering,

doing something for someone without telling anyone about it (It's such a temptation to let people know how *nice* I am.),

making friends instead of enemies,

saying I'm sorry when I really am but don't want to admit it,

appreciating others as much as I think they should appreciate me,

letting someone behind me (who is in a hurry) go ahead of me at the grocery check-out. (That isn't easy!)

Growing up means growing more kind, more friendly, more thoughtful, more generous, more compassionate, more cheerful, and more emotionally secure.

I can't help growing *old*—the step is slowing and the wrinkles are showing—but, God, give me grace (I need it) to grow *up* along with it.

Because growing *up* will probably mean the difference between happiness and bitterness while I am growing older. I do not want to be bitter. Bitter people are lonely people—and very unhappy people. Nor do I want to remain an emotional adolescent all my life.

Dear God,
As I older grow,
May I be childlike
In my love for Thee,
But never childish
In my actions toward others.
Keep my spirit young, God,
But help me to accept my years,
Knowing that every age
Has its own rewards.

19

Life Isn't *All* Downhill After 60

Don't ever let anyone tell you it is. Quite a few of my friends in the church have recreational vehicles (RVs to the camping crowd). In winter months they spurn our lovely Oregon rains for the desert sunshine of California or Arizona. While they are there, a number of them help different home mission stations with building and repairs. One couple, while on a visit to Hawaii, did the same thing there.

When I was 62, I started working as social director in the retirement residence where I lived at that time. I did this for two years and enjoyed it immensely.

I uncovered some abilities during that time that I didn't know I had. In school I hated art class. I was a dud in it. But umpteen years later I had fun making all sorts of

59

imaginative table favors and other doodads, as we called them, to use for parties and special holiday occasions. Some of these doodads are still cherished as souvenirs by my friends there.

I became interested in driftwood artistry—and even sold a few of my "productions."

When I was 65, I wrote my first book. Before that it had been only poems, stories, and articles. And I had written nothing for publication for over 20 years.

Most churches have an active senior citizen program. And there is Sunday School (I still tell Bible stories to the kids, on a guest basis, twice a month)—and the choir. I think the crazy poems they have me write for our get-togethers is the main reason they want me in the choir. There's also our missionary study group. There's really a lot for us "old people" to do—if we are interested.

If one is able—both physically and financially—to travel, now is the time. No formulas to formulate—no pampers to hamper!

By plane, by bus, by train, by car—by air, by sea, by land—look at the passengers and you'll find a passel of them over 60—some of them way over!

We really never get too old for new experiences. A young doctor friend in Kansas took me up in his plane last spring. It was my first ride in a small plane—and I loved it. He even let me handle the controls for a few minutes. I kept the plane level (I watched a little gauge on the board); but I had it climbing pretty steep, I guess, so I turned it back to him.

I can't drive a car. In fact, I never even drove a horse. Nor did I ever ride a bicycle. (I have problems enough keeping my balance when I'm on foot sometimes!)

But for a few thrilling moments, I flew a plane!

His mother (one of my former teenagers!) was with us, and she suggested that I write a poem about it. This is it.

Lift me up, Lord,
When life becomes
Just ordinary—
My days too much the same,
And nights for only sleeping—
Not for dreams.

Lift me up when I
Begin to notice
Only scars,
And not the glory
Of Your wondrous
World around me.

When life seems
Only hodgepodge
With no master plan,
Then lift me up
And let me see
The ordered beauty
Of field and meadow,
Brook and stream.
And help me see
That my life, too,
Is shaped and planned
By Thee.

When my heart needs warming,
My pulses stirred,
My vision made more keen,
Then lift me up, Lord,
Upon Thy wings of love,

And from the heights
I'll get a clearer view
Of all Thou hast
In store for me.

20

The Bus and I

I usually travel cross-country by bus, now that I am alone. I choose that mode of travel because it is cheaper, and, besides, I can see more scenery. I like to ride—and it gets me closer to my destination at the end than a plane does.

On the other hand, it is also dirtier, noisier, slower, more crowded, and much more uncomfortable. But the extra time it takes gives me opportunity to think deep thoughts—like, Is my entire lower body really paralyzed or has it just gone numb from sitting so long? A lot of the time I meditate on the joys of traveling by plane, or auto, or even ox-drawn covered wagon.

I once confided to my brother that, from observation, I had decided that the elite do not travel by bus. But the next time I'm overcome by wanderlust, there I am again.

I've really had some wonderful times riding the bus. I

remember a beautiful August evening in 1944. It was war-time and the bus was crowded. We pulled out of Salt Lake City just at dusk. Soon, three or four fellow travelers near me began singing. At first they sang songs popular that year—then (somewhat out of season) they started "Silent Night." I joined them. Then I led out with "I Come to the Garden Alone"—and they joined in. They wanted to sing more, so we sang "The Old Rugged Cross." Others around us started calling out requests and joined in: "Yield Not to Temptation," "Beulah Land"—the requests came thick and fast for those old-time songs of their Sunday School days. Some of the singers had really good voices. When someone started "When the Saints Go Marching In," it sounded like an old-fashioned camp meeting as everyone joined in.

We were at the front of a very long bus. The ones in the back could hear the singing but were too far away to follow us. So my daughter and a young couple back there started a sing-along of their own—in which others quickly joined. Soon the whole bus resounded with gospel singing as we rode through the darkness. We sang that way until midnight.

I've had some bad times too. Like when I get seated with someone as wide as I am. Before long we're like Siamese twins—one can't move without the other also moving.

On one of my jaunts to California, a lady boarded the bus and sat down beside me. Without even looking at her, I murmured, "These seats were designed for skinny midgets."

I was embarrassed when I looked up. She was the skinniest woman I ever saw.

I was passing through Colorado on the bus in the summer of 1949. We made a 15-minute rest stop at some little place there. The station was really just a house. The rest rooms were in another building which also housed a laundry room. The wife was doing her Monday wash there on the board with a huge tub of soap suds.

It had rained there recently, and the ground was very muddy. How muddy was it? It was so muddy that when I inadvertently stepped off the narrow boardwalk with one foot, I slithered full length in the slickest mud I ever saw.

No one even saw me as they kept scurrying along. And there I lay neglected, ignored, and *very* muddy. I yelled, "Well, look at me! Somebody just look at me!"

They looked—and fortunately they acted. They scooped me up out of that mud (none of *them* fell down), propelled me into the laundry room, and sudsed the mud off my new, gray, sharkskin suit in a trice. By the time the bus left—15 minutes later—I was as clean as a whistle, even to my shoes. No matter that I was still quite damp.

Thank You, God, for helping hands that always seem ready when I need them. And that is quite often. Where would I be without them? In that instance, still lying in some gooey Colorado mud, I reckon.

Once, in the wee hours of the morning the bus driver shook me awake. I'd been contorted into some semblance of a sleeping position in a double seat. Mine was the last available seat, and a passenger was getting on. I sat up, located my shoes, put them on, and moved over a notch. Then I went back to sleep until our breakfast stop in Bend, Ore.

After I'd eaten breakfast and walked around a bit, I sat down in the lobby to wait until the bus was ready to leave on the last leg of my journey. A lady who was sitting by me said admiringly, "I sure like your shoes."

I glanced down at them. Then I laughed. "They look even better when they are on the right feet." I'd got them on wrong when I was awakened on the bus and had been trotting around that way without noticing. (You see, before I begin a trip, I always buy a pair of shoes at least one size too big to allow for swelling while riding.)

On one bus trip, my daughter and I were riding from California to Kansas. It was during WW II and since so many were riding the bus, two sections were traveling together. Both were packed—people were even sitting in the aisles. After dark they stopped at a small cafe, so we got out and went in.

I returned to the bus ahead of my daughter, but when I got on, I couldn't remember which seat was mine. All I could see were sleeping bodies sprawled all over the place. I couldn't recognize *any* of them. But I hoped maybe some of them might recognize me and help me find the right seat. So I asked in a loud, clear voice, "Have any of you people ever seen me before?"

Those sleeping bodies jerked to attention, but no one said a word; they just *looked.*

Just then my daughter appeared at the door of the bus and said in a tone of patient resignation, "*Mother*, you're on the wrong bus."

Once, in later years, when coming home from the Midwest, there was some kind of a mix-up in Kansas City. (It *couldn't* have been my fault!) As a result, I came home on one bus, and my luggage on another—one day later. The day I got back, a small news item appeared on the evening menu sheet which caused a lot of merriment among the Cascade Manor residents. It read, "Audre Pitts arrived today without her clothes."

But, all in all, bus riding is an interesting experience. I've met people whom I would love to see again. And, of course, I have met a very few whom I wish I hadn't seen in the first place. If you want to see a cross section of humanity, then climb aboard!

A young college student who was riding all the way from New York to Corvallis, Ore., last summer expressed

66

his enjoyment of the scenery. He'd always flown before. He never realized how *big* our country was until he rode across it from "sea to shining sea" in a bus.

Another thing I like about it is that it gives me a chance to indulge in one of my favorite pastimes—people watching!

I'm a people-watching person;
    At the passing throng I stare:
People coming, people going—
    Busy people everywhere!

Short ones, fat ones,
    Slim ones and the tall,
The pretty and the plain ones—
    I like to watch them all.

When waiting for a bus or plane,
    A book I do not need;
I'd rather sit and people-watch—
    I can stay home and read.

I don't believe I'm nosey,
    And I never snoop or pry,
But I'm simply fascinated
    By the people passing by.

When I get to heaven—
    Where I'm going when I die—
I'll curl up on a fluffy cloud
    And people-watch in the sky.

21

Grandparents Are Special

Grandparents are very special people. If you don't think so, just ask their grandchildren.

Grandparents have warm laps and arms made especially for squeezing small children.

Grandparents are fun to sit with in church. They don't make you sit up quite so straight. And they can draw better pictures. Sometimes they have peppermint candy for you to eat when you get tired of listening to the preacher.

Grandmothers like to bake cookies. They like, even better, to have you eat them. And they don't scold when you accidentally spill your milk.

Grandfathers have strong legs that let you "ride a cock horse to Banbury Cross."

Grandparents like to buy presents for you—even when it isn't your birthday or Christmas.

Grandparents are always saying to parents, "He didn't mean to be naughty."

Grandparents are people who get accused (by parents) of spoiling their grandchildren.

Grandparents are the people who can tell you funny stories about your mom or your dad when they were little.

They even tell you about things they did when they were boys and girls. ("Were you really a boy once, Grandpa?")

Most grandparents wear glasses and sometimes they put little things in their ears so they can hear better.

Some of them can even take their teeth out to brush them. (That's neat!)

Grandparents have hardly any toys at their house, but they have other things that are fun to play with. Like potato mashers that grandmas don't use any more. They're great for squishing slugs!

And grandpas always have boards to pound nails into.

Grandparents know a lot of little songs and rhymes which they didn't always have time to tell *their* boys and girls. So they saved them all for you.

Grandparents are the nicest people in the whole world—next to mommies and daddies.

> *Grandparents*
> *Aren't like they*
> *Used to be—*
> *Grandma wears pantsuits,*
> *And Grandpa has a CB radio*
> *And a "handle."*
> *They are always going somewhere*
> *In their RVs;*
> *But when they get back home*
> *And hug you tight,*
> *You know they love you*
> *Just like real grandparents.*

22

Keeping the Spiritual Arteries Open

How tempting it is, as we grow older, to use our age as an excuse for some of the things we do—or don't do. But this is no time to rest on our laurels and reminisce.

I hope I never turn my brain out to pasture (as long as I have any control over it) or feed it on the chaff of television soap operas. It may not be much of a brain, but it's all I've got. I think it deserves better treatment than that.

Once in a Wednesday evening Bible study, our pastor made the statement that women seem to have stronger and better intuition than men. Guess who piped out, "That's what God gave us instead of a brain!" The men loved it but I almost got clobbered by the women afterward.

Age does not qualify one to be a spiritual freeloader. Neither does it guarantee grace.

It takes more than gray hair and wrinkled hands to be a mother in Israel. Or stooped shoulders and a cane to be a spiritual patriarch.

Some of my most beautiful friends are advanced in years. But they aren't really old, for they have kept their souls alive and their hearts full of joy. They are happy people and they spread happiness to others.

People who are really old (no matter how many or how few years they have lived) are the ones who sit around and feel sorry for themselves. They complain of being lonely. And with their whining complaints they drive away those who would befriend them. Then they become even more lonely and hopeless. Nothing will wrinkle the soul more quickly than self-pity.

Another soul-wrinkling habit (indulged in by people of *all* ages) is the habit of criticism and negative thinking. I know it takes more than just the power of positive thinking to be a victorious Christian, but if we are to be victorious, I'm positive our thinking will have to be positive.

Our attitudes reflect in our faces. A smiling face may not really make us more youthful-looking, but it's a lot more pleasant for other people to look at.

We can't help growing older in years—and our physical bodies will feel (and show) the effects of those years—but we need to keep our spiritual arteries unclogged. If we let complaining, self-pity, and all these negative emotions have full sway, they will destroy our happiness.

We need to keep our spiritual arteries open by prayer, praise, reading God's Word, love, laughter, compassion, and faith in God and in our fellow Christians (this last is *very* important). Then the sweet presence of the Holy Spirit can gladden our hearts and minds—and enrich our lives.

I'm getting older, God;
At least I've had
A lot of birthday cakes.
But I don't feel old
Inside.
It seems so short a time
Since I walked beside my father,
Dropping beans in hills,
For him to cover
With dark, moist earth;
Or when I tried to keep
From wiggling while
My mother combed my hair
In two black braids.
Now, when I look
In the mirror,
The face I see there
Is not the face I see
When I think of me.
Where did that little girl go?

23

Senile? Who, Me?

I'm glad I can laugh at myself. As a child I had a terrible inferiority complex. I didn't know it was a complex. I thought I really *was* inferior! (I hadn't learned yet that God doesn't make inferior people—or superior people either, for that matter. He just makes people. It's Satan who goes to work trying to make them feel either inferior or superior.)

I never laughed at myself then. Who could be cruel enough to laugh at a poor, little, know-nothing nobody like me? Now I can poke fun at myself without compunction. This doesn't damage my self-esteem in the least. It's only if I cry about myself in self-pity or brag about myself that I hurt myself.

Rather, a sense of humor places my faults and my foibles in proper perspective. I can acknowledge them—and still rather be me than anyone else in the world.

But I'm really *not* senile. Senility is what makes other people my age do funny things. I'm just an absent-minded, talkative saint-over-60 with a poor memory for names (and faces—and quite a few other things) who leaves her possessions scattered hither and yon, gets lost easily, never knows what day it is, and spends a lot of time wool-gathering.

Other people my age have a tendency to brag about their former abilities. I just want to give younger ones the benefit of my vast experience and superior wisdom!

Some grow conceited as they age, but I've just learned self-confidence through the years.

Some become a bit sharp-tongued. I'm witty (at least half witty).

Some get childish as they grow older. I'm just young at heart.

Some regress to their earlier years. I just have girlish charm. (Quit laughing.)

Some women wear bright colors to attract attention. I wear them to enhance my beauty. (It *needs* enhancing!)

Some people are senile. I'm interesting!

I must get my tongue out of my cheek before it gets stuck there!

> I don't know how it came about,
>   But, somehow, years ago
> One part of me grew up—matured,
>   The other part refused to grow.
>
> She's still a child, a sassy minx,
> Who often blurts out what she thinks.
>
> She spends my money foolishly
>   On useless trinkets, now and then;
> And, though I scold her solemnly,
>   I'm sure she'll do it soon again.

She makes me wear a bright red dress,
  Then we go tripping down the street.
I have stiff knees, but that gay child
  Wears scarlet sandals on her feet!

24

The Other Side of
the Mountain

I don't know how many of you grew up during the popularity of the song about the bear going over the mountain to see what he could see.

I'm on the other side of the mountain now, I guess. I didn't go just to see what I could see. But I did enjoy a lot of the sights along the way. I had a lot of fun going *up* the mountain (give or take a few rough spots) and I expect to have fun going down—give or take a few rough spots.

Middle age (I'll probably still consider myself *middle-aged* when I'm 90) is kind of like a favorite easy chair. It's all hollowed out to fit you in all the right spots. You can settle down in it and rock along at a slower pace. That is, unless you're breaking your neck trying to prove you're still young.

I'm not recommending that we literally retire into our easy chairs. God has work for all of us. But He doesn't expect us all to do the same work—or at the same speed.

Middle age is sort of like traveling over a familiar road. You know where a lot of the bumps and chuckholes are, and it's easier to avoid them. Some can't be avoided. All you can do is brace yourself for the jolt. Even that becomes easier with practice.

It's like a pair of comfortable old shoes that have been well broken in through the years.

It's when you begin to think about the quality of your life instead of the quantity of your possessions.

It's a time of beginning to let go of some of the material things you thought you couldn't live without.

It should be a time of deeper consecration, more time for the reading of the Word, and a closer walk with God in prayer.

As I said, I had fun going up the mountain, but I wouldn't want to go back and climb it again—even if I had the chance.

On this side of the mountain I can see the slanting rays of the distant sunset. (Some days I hope it is *far* distant; on others I look at it with longing.) I see its brilliance touching the autumn landscape with red and gold.

On this side of the mountain I am seeing the fruition of the labors of many consecrated sowers of the seed. I have watched the growth of young Christians beside whom I knelt at an altar of prayer when they first sought God. I have seen them mature into wonderful Christian parents—and grandparents.

I have seen churches planted where there were no churches, and have watched them reach out into their communities—winning souls for Christ. I have watched them grow—and outgrow—their facilities, then build bigger ones, and outgrow them.

I have seen friends pass through deep sorrows and tragedies, and become stronger Christians—not because of the sorrows, but because of their constant trust in God during those times.

I have seen a lot of things. But never once have I seen God fail even one of His children.

It is autumn on the hillsides,
The October of my life;
The fresh, clean air
Is sweet with the
Fragrance of heaven's promise;
The sunset beckons me.
But I would not leave the harvest field
Until my work is done,
And only God can know
When that will be.
Then He will come and walk along with me
The rest of the way home.

25

I Want to Live ... Now

I do not agree with those who would assure us that if we have hobbies and friends and stay socially active, we will never grow old or sick or senile. Neither do I agree with those who tell us that if we are really committed to the Lord, we will be spared from every illness—from rickets to arthritis to nerve disorders.

From my nonmedical, nontheological soap box I would proclaim that I have often seen it work otherwise. In spite of hobbies and religion people get sick and die. And never once in the Bible do I find where Jesus condemned anyone for being sick.

Some step suddenly from this world into the next. If they are children of God, this is a most blessed way to go. But others linger on—Christian and non-Christian sharing the same fate (and sometimes even the same nursing home room). Some become completely disoriented in their minds. These tear our hearts and we pray that we and those we love may be spared from this. But we are promised no choices.

Neither would I agree with those (and I'm sure I've been in that number in the past) who say that God knows just what we need to get to heaven and will send only the trials and sickness we need to get us there. To a degree, yes. He knows what lessons we need to learn and how to draw us closer to himself.

But I believe He has a higher purpose for our lives than just to get us to heaven—as glorious as that will be. I have friends who, I am convinced, could make it to heaven with a lot less physical suffering than they are enduring. And others, who are living deeply consecrated lives, face many crushing tragedies.

I don't profess to know the mind of God. Perhaps He wants to use us in this way to be a blessing to others, that He, through our suffering, may win souls to himself. In that case I gladly say, "Use me, Lord."

Another theory which I can't accept is that God chooses only the strong ones to bear heavy burdens and spares the weak. I've heard people say, "I guess the reason God has spared me these things is that He knows I couldn't take it."

I cannot picture a loving God sitting on His royal throne, scanning the universe, sorting out the strong upon whom He can drop a heavy burden, from those whom He must spare because of their delicate spiritual condition.

Not all trials come from God—and no one is strong when he is under pressure. Likewise, no one is weak when he avails himself of God's strength.

We must never try to carry our burdens alone. We must never try to prove our strength just because we are Christians and are supposed to have a lot of faith. Our only hope is to ask God to help us carry the load. And then a loving God lifts us up in His fatherly arms and carries both us and our burden!

What I was saying (before I got carried away) is that hobbies, interests, friends, active participation in church, and a totally consecrated life will not magically protect us from accidents or sickness—either in old age or youth. (Have I told you this before?)

But I can guarantee that we will be happier now if we have those interests. And *now* is all we really have. We are daily absorbing our future into our *Now!*

Dear God, as I leaf through
The pages of my life,
I find that the chapters
Covering my past
Are many.
I skip past the Now
And turn to read my future;
But I find only blank, empty pages,
And I have no way of knowing
How many will be filled.
I turn back to the Now—
It is all I have,
And all I really need—
As long as I have You, God.

26

P.S. to Teens

How can you be happy when you get older? That's easy—be happy now.

If you want to be pleasant-looking when you are older—put on a happy face now.

Smile—not only because God loves you, but because you are setting your countenance in the mold that it will always have.

If you insist on being selfish and having your own way in your formative years, even God will have a problem getting you out of it later.

Griping is a habit—and not a pleasant one at that. Have you been around older people who seemingly griped about everything? They probably formed the habit when they were kids.

Happiness can be a habit too—and it's a lot more fun. Cultivate the happiness habit.

Want to have lots of friends—now and later on? Be friendly. It says in Proverbs, "In order to have friends, a man must show himself friendly." Makes sense, doesn't it?

You've got a lot of livin' to do before you make it to your old age. Don't waste the years—enjoy them. Commit them to God. Let Him be your constant Companion. Do you admire some special older Christian and wish you were like that? Start today to follow their pattern. Time flies.

> *You're writing a book,*
> *And you are the hero*
> *Or heroine;*
> *You're staging a play,*
> *And you are the star;*
> *You're painting a picture,*
> *A self-portrait of you;*
> *You're making a sculpture,*
> *The image is yours;*
> *You're writing a song,*
> *Your deeds are the grace notes;*
> *You're building a future*
> *With bricks marked "Today."*